Nature 1

How many ...?

1 **Unscramble the questions. Then answer.**

1 favourite / animal / your / is / What

_____

_____

2 your / is / colour / What / favourite

_____

_____

2 **Read. Then find two questions and two answers.**

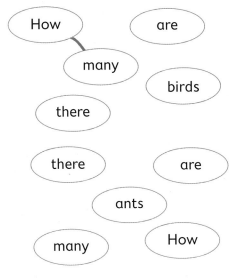

How   are   There

many   are

birds   thirty

there

there   are   are

ants   three

many   How   There

1 <u>How many</u> _____   _____

2 _____   _____

3 **Look. Then read and match.**

1	Are there any insects?	a	Yes, there are. There are three.
2	Is there a tree?	b	No, there aren't.
3	Are there any frogs?	c	Yes, there is. There is one.

4 **Read and complete. Use *is*, *are*, *isn't* or *aren't*.**

The frog

In my garden there ¹_____ a pond. It's not a big pond but there ²_____ some fish and frogs in it. I go to the pond to play with my boat. There ³_____ one frog that is my favourite. It swims next to my boat. Sometimes it jumps out of the pond onto the rocks. There ⁴_____ any clouds in the sky today. It is very hot, it ⁵_____ cold. There ⁶_____ three frogs there today.

5 Unscramble the questions.

1 are / Where / from / you

_____

2 your / do / friends / Where / you / with / play

_____

3 go / you / holiday / Where / on / do

_____

4 bag / Where / your / is / school

_____

6 Read. Then order the dialogue.

- [ ] **a** I'm from Seville. It's in the south of Spain. Where are you from?
- [ ] **b** Really? Happy birthday! How old are you?
- [ ] **c** I'm Freddie. Where are you from?
- [ ] **d** I'm from Córdoba. It's in Argentina. It's my birthday today.
- [ ] **e** I was born in May. My birthday is next month. Let's go to the beach to play.
- [ ] **f** I'm 11. When were you born?
- [ ] **g** Great!
- [1] **h** Hi, I'm Sam. What's your name?

2 Me

I've got ... have got

1 Read and underline four mistakes. Then write.

I got black hair. My sister have got black hair, too. I hasn't got glasses. Have got you long hair?

I've got _____

_____

_____

_____

_____

2 Draw. Then write about you. Use some of the words in the box.

have got	haven't got
short	nose	long
hair	chin	eyes
round	glasses	thick
neck	eyebrows	small

_____

_____

_____

_____

3 Draw lines in different colours. Make sentences.

I Jamie Claire and Stuart	have got has got	a big small green short black	beard eyes hair

4 Unscramble sentences. Then colour.

1 got / Jenny / hair / long / has / brown

_____

_____

2 has / Steve / got / hair / short / black

_____

_____

3 got / Helena / blue / has / eyes / small

_____

_____

4 big / has / George / got / ears

_____

_____

2 Have you got ... ?

⑤ Read. Then answer.

Personal information

Have you got long/short hair?	I've got
What colour hair have you got?	
What colour eyes have you got?	
Have you got glasses?	
Have you got a beard?	
Have you got a moustache?	

⑥ Read. Then complete. Use *have got*.

Me

Hi, I'm Sally. This is a photo of my family. I ¹ **have** got one sister and one brother. I ²_____ got short hair, I've got long hair. In this photo, my brother has ³_____ a ball. He loves football. His name is Craig. My sister and mum ⁴_____ got long blond hair. We haven't ⁵_____ thick eyebrows but we ⁶_____ got small ears. My dad ⁷_____ got a beard or a moustache but my grandad has. I love my family!

Pets 3

What does it look like?

1 **Read. Then match and write.**

1 It's got wings. It hasn't got feathers. It's got six legs. It's different colours.

2 It's got two feet and it's got claws. It's different colours. It's got a tail. It hasn't got four legs.

3 It's green. It hasn't got fur or hair. It's got four long legs.

4 It's got a lot of fur and long whiskers. It's got a small white tail and very big ears.

a    **b**    **c**    **d**

It's a butterfly. _____   _____   _____

2 **Read. Then circle.**

1 Have *he* / (*you*) got a pet?

2 Yes I *have* / *haven't*. I have got a rabbit.

3 What *does* / *do* it look like?

4 My cat *has* / *have* got brown paws. It *has* / *have* got short ears.

3 Have you got ...?

3 Look and answer.

Ben	✘	✘	✘	✔	✘
Sam	✘	✔	✔	✘	✘
Gemma	✔	✔	✘	✘	✔
Pamela	✔	✘	✔	✘	✔
	tortoise	hamster	rabbit	snake	parrot

1 Has Sam got a rabbit and a tortoise?
   No, he hasn't. He's got a rabbit and a hamster.

2 Has Pamela got a snake?

   _____

3 Have Sam and Gemma got hamsters?

   _____

4 Has Ben got a rabbit?

   _____

5 Have Gemma and Pamela got a tortoise?

   _____

6 Has Sam got two pets?

   _____

7 Have Pamela and Gemma got four pets?

   _____

4 Look again at Activity 3. Then write four true sentences.
Use *have / haven't got*.

   1 _____

   2 _____

   3 _____

   4 _____

5 Look. Then circle.

Emma

Paul

1 Emma's got a rabbit *(but)* / *and* she hasn't got a snake.

2 Paul hasn't got a parrot *but* / *and* he has got two frogs.

3 Emma's got a dog *but* / *and* Paul's got a dog.

4 Emma's got two cats *but* / *and* a parrot.

5 They haven't got a fish *but* / *and* they have got a dog.

6 Look at Activity 5. Read and complete. Use the words from the box.

| cats | and | got | wings | has | but |

This is Emma and Paul. They've ¹ _got_ lots of pets. Emma has got five pets and Paul ² _____ got five pets, too. Paul has got a dog ³ _____ Emma has got a dog. The parrot has got ⁴ _____ and a beak. It's a beautiful bird. The ⁵ _____ have got long whiskers ⁶ _____ the snake hasn't.

4 Home

It's next to ...

1 Look and unscramble. Then write and ✔ or ✘.

1 TV / opposite / The / is / chair / the

_____

2 three / plants / in / The / front / window / are / of / the

_____

3 four / in / are / There / cats / living room / the

_____

2 Read the answer. Then write a question about your house.

1 Is the TV next to the sofa? _____ Yes, it is.

2 _____ No, they aren't.

3 _____ Yes, they are.

4 _____ No, it isn't.

3 Read the letter. Then circle.

Hi Claire,

What does your new house look like? ¹(Is)/ Are there a balcony?
²Is / Are there any ³plant / plants on the balcony? I love plants!
⁴Is / Are there a basement?

What does the garden look like? ⁵Are / Is it big? ⁶Is / Are there a garage? ⁷Is / Are the cars in the garage?

Send me a photo.

Love, Beth

4 Write a letter about your home. Use the words in the box.

| wardrobe | plants | basement | bedrooms |
| picture | mirrors | big garden | garage |

_____

_____

_____

_____

_____

4 Revision

5 Look. Then write. Use the grid.

There	is	a	plant(s)	in	the	TV
	are	two	wardrobe(s)	on		wardrobe
		three	sofa(s)	under		balcony
		lots of	lamp(s)	above		garden
			car(s)	opposite		garage
			food	behind		basement
			table(s)	next to		cupboard
			chair(s)			sofa
						chair
						table

1 <u>There is a sofa next to the TV.</u>

2 _____

3 _____

4 _____

5 _____

6 _____

6 Draw your classroom. Then write.

_____

_____

_____

_____

_____

_____

_____

Clothes

What are you wearing?

1 Read the messages. Then answer.

> What are you wearing to Fran's party after school?
> Are you wearing your new trainers?

> I'm wearing black jeans, a brown leather belt and a red and white T-shirt.

> Are you wearing your new trainers?

> No, I'm not.
> I'm wearing my old white trainers.
> I love those trainers.
> What are you wearing?

> I'm wearing yellow and green shorts and I'm wearing a red hat. It's my favourite baseball hat.
> Is Jenny wearing new boots?

> Yes, she is. They are really nice.
> Okay. I've got Maths now.
> See you after school. Bye.
> Kate x

> Okay. See you at 3.30.
> Becky x

1 What is Becky wearing to the party?

_____

2 Is Kate wearing her new trainers?

_____

3 Is Jenny wearing her new boots?

_____

4 What is Kate wearing with her jeans?

_____

2 Find the question and answer.

What	am	?	She's	wearing	a	is	but
is →	Kate	wearing	white	and	red	brown	belt
and	there	this	T-shirt	.	a	is	leather

5 **This is ... / These are ...**

3 **Read. Then write.**

| old jeans | a green T-shirt | a brown beanie | flip flops |
| a blue belt | white sandals | a woolly jumper | cotton shorts |

This is ...	These are ...
a green T-shirt	

4 **Read. Then circle.**

1 *This is /* (*These are*) my new jeans.

2 *This is / These are* my favourite skirt.

3 This *is / are* my favourite blouse.

4 These are my brown *shorts / skirt*.

5 **Draw your favourite clothes. Then write. Use** *this is / these are.*

_____
_____
_____
_____
_____
_____
_____

6 **Draw. Then write.**

Ben	Sue
	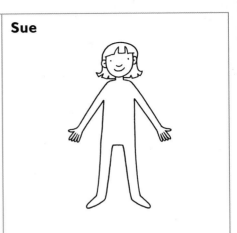

Ben <u>is wearing</u> _____

_____

Sue <u>is wearing</u> _____

_____

7 **Read. Then complete. Use words from the word box.**

> made is wool is am wearing are black wearing from

I ^{1}<u>am</u> ^{2}<u>wearing</u> a brown leather jacket.

What a great T-shirt. It ^{3}_____ ^{4}_____ of cotton. It's blue and white.

Georgie ^{5}_____ wearing ^{6}_____ trousers. They ^{7}_____ made ^{8}_____ cotton.

What a beautiful jumper! Andrew's ^{9}_____ a white jumper. It's made from ^{10}_____ .

6 Sports
can / can't

1 Look. Then answer.

Class survey of different sports

	1	2	3	4	5
20					
15				■	
10			■	■	
5	■	■	■	■	■
	Ride a bike	Do taekwondo	Play tennis	Play football	Play volleyball

1 How many children can ride a bike?

<u>Twenty children can ride a bike.</u>

2 Can fifteen children play football?

_____

3 How many children can play volleyball?

_____

4 Can ten children play tennis?

_____

5 Can ten children do taekwondo?

_____

2 Write about you. What sports can or can't you do?

_____

_____

_____

3 Look. Then write sentences. Use the prompts.

My	gym	✘	skating rink	✔
My dad	stadium	✔	beach	✘
My best friend	ski slope	✘	gym	✔
My aunt	house	✘	park	✔
My mum	gym	✔	kitchen	✘
My teacher	football pitch	✘	beach	✔

1 I wasn't at the gym. I was at the skating rink.

2 My dad _____

3 My best friend _____

4 My aunt _____

5 _____

6 _____

4 Complete the table.

Last weekend, I was ...	Last weekend, I wasn't ...

5 Read and draw or write.

1 Stretch your arms up.

2 Bend your knees.

3 _____

4 Twist your body to the right.

5 _____

6 Jump.

Do you like ...?

1 **Read and ✔ or ✗. Then write questions and answers.**

spinach _____	✔
lettuce _____	☐
tomatoes _____	☐

strawberries _____	☐
mangoes _____	☐
peaches _____	☐

1 <u>Do you like spinach?</u> <u>Yes I do.</u>

2 _____ _____

3 _____ _____

4 _____ _____

5 _____ _____

6 _____ _____

2 **Unscramble. Find the questions and answers.**

1 broccoli / I / do / Do / like / you / Yes

_____ _____

2 like / No / Sam / doesn't / Does / he / apricots

_____ _____

3 Yes / Tina / cherries / does / she / Does / like

_____ _____

7 Is / Are there any ...?

3 **Read. Then complete.**

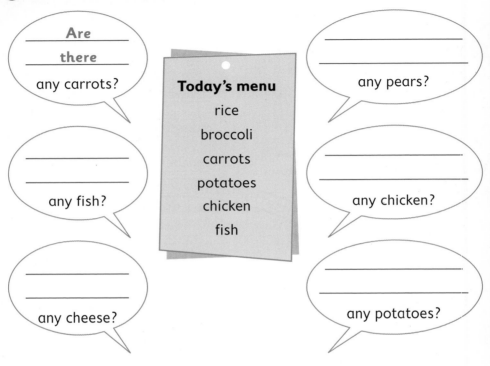

_____Are_____
_____there_____
any carrots?

Today's menu
rice
broccoli
carrots
potatoes
chicken
fish

_____
_____
any pears?

_____
_____
any fish?

_____
_____
any chicken?

_____
_____
any cheese?

_____
_____
any potatoes?

4 **Read the answers. Look at Activity 3. Then write the questions.**

1 _Is there any fish?_____

Yes, there is.

2 _____

No, there isn't.

3 _____

No, there aren't.

4 _____

Yes, there are.

5 **Read and sort the food into *some* and *lots of*. Then write.**

plums   lettuce   cucumber   beans   broccoli
cabbage   oranges   watermelon   mangoes
apricots   avocadoes   papaya   cherries

There is some ...	There are lots of ...
lettuce	plums

6 **Read. Then unscramble and write.**

1 lots / on / There / potatoes / are / the / table / of

_____

2 in / is / fridge / cabbage / the / There / some

_____

3 lots / on / of / are / plate / peaches / the / There

_____

4 some / the / There / in / pan / is / fish

_____

8 Things we do

What are you doing?

➊ Read. Then answer.

1 What are Jane and Sue doing? (*read / library*)
<u>They are reading in the library.</u>

2 What is Tom doing? (*play football / stadium*)

_____

3 What is Karen doing? (*watch TV / living room*)

_____

4 What are you doing now?

_____

➋ Look. Then write.

my sister   my brother

my dad   my grandparents

1 sister, read <u>My sister is reading a book in the bedroom.</u>

2 brother, wash _____

3 dad, drink _____

4 grandparents, talk _____

3 Read and complete.

1 <u>Are you playing the violin? No, I am not.</u>

2 _____ (do / homework)

3 _____ John _____ ? (sing / loudly)

4 Yes, he _____ .

5 _____ ? (you / work)

4 Find the mistakes. Then correct.

1 I (is) playing on my computer in my bedroom.
   <u>I am playing on my computer in my bedroom.</u>

2 It are raining outside.
   _____

3 Mum reading the book.
   _____

4 Dad are walking in the park.
   _____

5 Grandad is sleep in his chair.
   _____

6 My dog is play with a ball.
   _____

8 Revision

5 Draw you and your friends. Then write. What are you doing? Use the words from the box.

watch	play	wash	drink	clean	sleep	eat
walk	run	dance	read	make	quickly	
loudly	quietly	slowly	terribly			

_____
_____
_____
_____
_____

6 Read then circle. Which one is not correct?

1 I'm reading a book. / I'm write a story. / Mum is eating.

2 Jo is watching TV. / Jo and Tom are dancing. / Jo are playing football.

3 Dad is washing the car. / Mum are doing taekwondo. / I am sleeping on the sofa.